Dear Parents and Educators,

Welcome to Penguin Young Readers! As parents and educators, you know that each child develops at their own pace—in terms of speech, critical thinking, and, of course, reading. Penguin Young Readers recognizes this fact. As a result, each Penguin Young Readers book is assigned a traditional easy-to-read level (1–4) as well as a Guided Reading Level (A–P). Both of these systems will help you choose the right book for your child. Please refer to the back of each book for specific leveling information. Penguin Young Readers features esteemed authors and illustrators, stories about favorite characters, fascinating nonfiction, and more!

Xavier Riddle and the Secret Museum: I am Cleopatra

LEVEL **3**

GUIDED READING LEVEL **K**

This book is perfect for a **Transitional Reader** who:
- can read multisyllable and compound words;
- can read words with prefixes and suffixes;
- is able to identify story elements (beginning, middle, end, plot, setting, characters, problem, solution); and
- can understand different points of view.

Here are some **activities** you can do during and after reading this book:
- Compound Words: A compound word is made when two words are joined together to form a new word. *Supermoon* is a compound word that is used in this story. Reread the story and try to find other compound words.
- Problem/Solution: In this story, Xavier wants to stay up past his bedtime to see the supermoon. This is the problem. The solution to this problem is learning how to ask his parents the right way. Discuss another problem in this story and the solution.

Remember, sharing the love of reading with a child is the best gift you can give!

*Penguin Young Readers are leveled by independent reviewers applying the standards developed by Irene Fountas and Gay Su Pinnell in *Matching Books to Readers: Using Leveled Books in Guided Reading*, Heinemann, 1999.

PENGUIN YOUNG READERS
An Imprint of Penguin Random House LLC, New York

Published in 2020 by Penguin Young Readers, an imprint of Penguin Random House LLC, New York.
Manufactured in China.

Visit us online at www.penguinrandomhouse.com.

ISBN 9780593096338 (pbk)   10 9 8 7 6 5 4 3 2 1
ISBN 9780593096406 (hc)   10 9 8 7 6 5 4 3 2 1

I am Cleopatra

adapted by Brooke Vitale

Tonight there will be
a supermoon in the sky.
Xavier wants to see it.

There is just one problem.
Xavier will have to stay up
past his bedtime.

He does not know how to ask
his parents.

This is a *big* problem.

It is time for the Secret Museum.

The friends find a coin

in the Secret Museum.

One side shows a girl's face.

"I wonder who that is," Brad says.

Just then they see a figure.

It is Cleopatra!

The coin must be hers.

"And we're meeting her in Egypt," Yadina says.

The friends put their hands
on Berby.
They travel back more than
2,000 years!

The friends see a cat.

"I see you found my cat,"

a voice says.

It is Cleopatra!

Cleopatra tells the friends
that she wants to go
to a big festival that day.

"I have to ask my dad if I can miss my afternoon lesson," she says.

"I really want to see a supermoon,"
Xavier says.

16

"But I have to ask my parents
if I can stay up past bedtime.
How are you going to ask your dad?"

Cleopatra stands up straight.
"I'll be prepared, confident,
and polite."

Cleopatra waves for the friends
to follow her.
"I'll teach you!"

"Be prepared and explain
what you want," she says.
The friends nod.
That makes sense.

"Be confident," Cleopatra says, "and speak clearly!"

"Be polite," Cleopatra says.

"Say please and thank you."

Xavier raises his hand.

"What happens if they say no?"

"No means no," Cleopatra says.
"But try to think of *why* they'd say no,
and come up with an idea
to help them say yes."

"I'll show you!"

It is time to ask her dad

if she can go to the festival.

"I'd like to go to the festival,"
she says.
"I think it will be good for me
as a future queen."

The king is not sure.

But Cleopatra is prepared.

"What if I take two hours

of lessons tomorrow,

instead of just one?"

Xavier holds his breath.

Finally, the king nods.

"Thank you, Dad!" Cleopatra says.

Back at home,
Xavier is finally ready
to ask his parents
about staying up late,
like Cleopatra taught him.

"I know that bedtimes are important," Xavier says. "So, what if we go to bed an hour earlier tomorrow?"

"Now *that* is a supermoon,"

Xavier says.

Yadina looks up at the moon.

"I think tomorrow I'll ask for a cat."